THE FIRE THAT NEVER GOES OUT

Other Books by Tom Furniss

Poetry

Triple Measures - Coverstory books, 2020

A Kind of Making - Coverstory books, 2019

Play for Three Hands - co-author, pamphlet, 1981

Non-fiction

Edmund Burke's Aesthetic Ideology: Language, Gender and Political Economy in Revolution - Cambridge University Press, 1993, 2008

Discovering the Footsteps of Time: Geological Travel Writing about Scotland, 1700-1820 - Edinburgh University Press, 2018, 2019

Ways of Reading: Advanced Reading Skills for Students of English Literature - co-author - Routledge, 1992, 2000, 2007, 2012

Reading Poetry: An Introduction - co-author, Longman, 1996, Pearson, 2007, Routledge 2012, 2018

Reading Poetry: A Complete Coursebook - co-author, Routledge 2022

TOM FURNISS

THE FIRE THAT NEVER GOES OUT: NEW POEMS

First published in paperback format by Coverstory books, 2024

ISBN 978-1-7384693-3-8

Copyright © Tom Furniss 2024

The right of Tom Furniss to be identified as the author of this work has been asserted by him in accordance with the Copyright, Designs and Patents Act 1988.

The cover image is based on a photograph taken by the author.

All rights reserved.

No part of this publication may be reproduced, circulated, stored in a system from which it can be retrieved, or transmitted in any form without the prior permission in writing of the publisher.

www.coverstorybooks.com

To Jason, my best reader

Contents

ON TIME IN PLACE
Written on a Tree 5
On Watling Street 7
Eastcote Revisited 9
The Sound of Chainsaws 12
Such a Night as This 13
High Wind in High Trees 14
Lines Written on Blank Pages of Gary Snyder's Riprap and Cold Mountain Poems Standing Beside Our Dry Stone Wall, Half Rebuilt 15
Haiku Days 17
Aidan's Haiku 18
A Flock of Rooks 19
The Fire that Never Goes Out 21

ON PEOPLE IN TIME
My Father's War 27
Like Father, Like Son 29
Remember, Remember 30
Lookalikes 32
For Jason: My Close Reader 34
A Season's Greetings Card from Jason and Waltraud, Christmas 2019 35
First Love, 1970 37
Burning Memories 40
To STC Again 41
Two Chained Sonnets 43
Wish You Were Here 44
Rebuilding a Dry-stone Wall 46
In Memoriam: Kenneth McNeil (20 March 1925 - 16 February 2021) 50
John 54

LOCKDOWN TIME
April Moon, 2020 60
Glen Lyon, October 2020 62
The Gift of Poetry 65
Spring 2021 67
Ash to Ash 69
Mycorrhizal Fungi 74

MOMENTS OF BEING

On An Ordinary August Day ... 79
Magnetic Movements ... 80
Winter ... 81
Golden River ... 82
On Listening Once Again to Beethoven's Piano Concerto No.4 ... 83
Poem Craft ... 84
Sonnet ... 85
Tree ... 86
Blane Water ... 88
Climbing Trees ... 89
Autumn In the Garden of Delight ... 91

JUST MY FUN

Big Shots ... 95
For the Birds ... 97
Compost ... 99
A Knight's Strange Night ... 100

❉

Acknowledgements ... 103

ON TIME IN PLACE

Written on a Tree

One hundred yards from where the child
I once was used to live,
Three hundred and fifty miles from now,
Four steps from tarmac path and Banbury Lane,
Just beyond a five-barred gate,
A tiny scrap of unused land,
Ten square yards at most,
In the corner of a farmer's field
That ploughs will never reach,
Set aside reluctantly
Long before grants,
A minute wasteland running wild,
Too small to mark on maps,
Hedged in with thorns, enclosed,
Unseen by passers-by, unheard
Save for nesting birds and whisperings,
A dwelling place for boys on the run
To find their inside selves and make abode,
Hide-out, refuge, shelter,
Site of trespass under scrap-land trees –
An ancient stunted slow-grown holly,
A horse chestnut whose spike-less shells
Enclose sabino half-formed conkers
Never fit for fights, with bark
Scored through with old penknife
To inner wood that dripped with sap,
Three centred rows of capitals
In lines of two and one and two,
Open wounds that never fully healed,
Whose scars could still be read

If ever readers stopped to lean
Against that gate and wondered
At that nook of untilled earth,
Climbed five bars and pushed
Through thorns to find themselves
Inside a sanctum for the lost
Boys or girls that they once were.
Such readers – there are none – could tell
Us what those letters say today:
The first three I know still – TF and L –
The last two I forget; no matter,
They would not summon name or face
Out of the wasteland of memory,
She was never scored into my heart.
I was twelve and practicing
My art.

On Watling Street

Watling Street ran past my gran's front door,
Two strides away, so close the traffic shook
The window where I watched the world go past
Along the eastern frontier of my life, heading
South and north beyond the compass of
Comprehension, broad grass trackway used
By Ancient Britons, stone-paved and metalled
By Roman legionnaires perhaps from Africa
Who tramped this way before my gran was born,
Beyond the dawn of time, marching north
To build a wall to keep barbarians
At bay and gaze out onto wilderness,
Or south towards Londinium,
Outpost of Roman power at a ford
Of the Thames. As I gazed in the early '60s
Through those small, framed squares of old
Uneven glass, warping space and time,
In Fosters Booth – where long ago a forester
Built his hut beside the turnpiked way, cutting
A clearing that would grow into a row
Of rowdy inns (only two remained) –
I saw cars go by only seen in films today
And post-war lorries wheezing up the hill
And vanishing beyond the northern rim
Of the world. My mother's mother sleeps
The sleep of one who's worked on hands and knees
To clean the steps of those who've risen high
In the eyes of the world. My mother's father talks
In his sleep as coals in the fire grate settle,
Grumble and grow older as I watch

The passers-by who barely glance at this
Undistinguished rented terraced house
In a red brick row, two up, two down,
An outdoor toilet out the back beyond
The braying pump and washing line.
The lead-blackened range roasts
Sunday beef and boils water drawn
From the depths in soot-encrusted kettle
Whistling on the hob. A wound-up clock
Unwinds the time in seconds and years
And time runs back and forth at will.

Passing from time to time
In years to come along this Roman way
I'll gaze through films of memory
At this renovated house whose occupants
Have never heard the names of those who passed
That threshold long ago between
The living and the dead, the worn-down step
Of stone eroded by the elements
And brush and elbow grease and pride
And passing feet of those who went before
And paid their dues, that single step between
Their inner life and passing world. And later still
I'll write these words that move me
Back and forth in time.

Eastcote Revisited

Rain falls soft on Eastcote,
Middle of Northamptonshire,
In the middle of the night,
Wife and child asleep nearby,
A tourist in a village where
I first kissed girls, drank beer,
Plucked Christmas turkeys on a farm.

No one knows me here today,
A stranger in a place that knows me not,
A paying guest in a B&B,
Like those ramblers following waymarked paths,
Clutching guides and maps and GPS.

Here in the dark I navigate in memory
The secret paths and ancient ways
Through fields and forests
Of my past.

In olden times Pound Lane
Led to a roadside pound
On Banbury Lane
Where cattle were penned
In a strip of land
That's still hedged round,
On the hoof from the Highlands
En route to Banbury Market,
Their journey's end.

When I was a boy Pound Lane,
Cutting between fields of memory,
Was lined with elms much older
Than me; I saw them felled
In their prime before their time,
Struck with disease. Since then
I've always known I'm older than
The trees that line that lane.

I walk Pound Lane in memory,
Cross Banbury Lane and climb
A gate and then I'm free to roam
The landscape of the past.

I used to follow unmarked ways,
Traces of paths in common use
In olden times through fields of green
And gold, plotting ancient routes
By what remained, half hidden
Rotten posts, rough-hewn
Narrow bridges crossing
Ditches and streams, gaps
In hedges, crooked stiles unused
For years, patterns of belief
And memories mapped in mind
And on this land, imagination
Rambling free, seeking solitude
In rare surviving corners where
Ploughs and cattle couldn't reach,
Where hedgerows met and streams
Meandered spanned by fallen trees.

I saw a fox one day across a field
Watching me watching him,
Still as the ripening corn in summer air,
Trespassing like me. It still sits there,
In memory and in these lines,
Along with all those other foxes
That have passed and pass
In and out of poetry.

The Sound of Chainsaws

The sound of chainsaws every day
In neighbours' gardens, crash of trees
Onto the earth that nourished them
And they all strove to rise above
To brush the sky of passing clouds
And thrash the wind with whiplash boughs;
The smell of broken pine and scent
Of wounded wood, of smoke and ash,
Tinged with the tang of memories
Unremembered all these years
Of watching long-forgotten men,
Rural working men with saws,
My father in his manhood then,
Cutting down and cutting up
An old great oak in a neighbour field,
The sawdust smell, sweet and moist,
Men who knew not what they did
But knew their trade and use of tools,
Felling trees and grubbing up
The hedgerows one by one where kids
Nested, hid, and foraged for food,
Last vestiges of wilderness,
Places for the play of mind
And habitude of memory.

The saws have fallen silent now
The men are long gone to their rest.
In the dead of sleepless nights
I miss the ghostly call of owls.

Such a Night as This

The neon glow of Glasgow to the south
Beyond the ridge of our glacial strath
Obscures the stars of half the sky,
Campsie Fells loom to the north
Brooding on their dreams of deep time,
Volcanic power poised as solid waves of rock,
Place of buzzards, falcons, rooks
Slicing the air and the last light of day,
A full moon swinging in eternal dance
At colossal speed with its partner Earth
Barely moving to the human eye
In year-long endless orbits round the Sun;
Bluebells, broom, and may exhaling
Breath of scents long held throughout a long hot day,
New remembered sound of rain on leaves
Of all the trees except the ash
Dying back, except the oak
Slow to leaf, slow to grow,
Outliving them all and all of this,
All this, gathered in words,
Scattered across the upper half of one blank page
Of the Penguin *War and Peace*
Under the spell of Natasha's dance
To Russian folk songs after the hunt
Of wolf and fox and hare in the woods
With horse and hound and lust for blood,
Blood up, blood spilled and blooded boys,
Natasha dancing on such a night as this
Far off in time and space and fictional
And yet right here right now and just as real.

High Wind in High Trees

High wind in high trees sounds
Like seventh waves breaking
On shingle, clouds to the north
Of the northern hills extend
Like snow-capped Alps beyond the rim of sight,
Tall summer grasses roll like the sea,
Dance among
Billions of photons arriving here at last
From the Sun, surfing their own waves,
Photosynthesis shimmering in leaves,
Pumping oxygen into air and lungs,
Pulsing through veins,
Waves of various frequencies
Vibrate in eyes and ears, radiate
Across the wildlife loch
That ripples like summer grass
Where contrary winds play chase,
Aquatic birds are ruffled, shepherding their young,
Invisible larks spirit themselves in the high-lit sky,
Ascend on the high wind and sing
Of all our summer yesterdays,
And bog myrtle scent summons
Memories of days on those northern hills,
And memories of days like these
      in days to come
           will come
   through words like these.

Lines Written on Blank Pages of Gary Snyder's *Riprap and Cold Mountain Poems* Standing Beside Our Dry Stone Wall, Half Rebuilt

an old cold rising sun enlightens
mountains to the north
lava flows solidified in time
scoured by glaciers
sitting quietly now
thousands of years and years
in zazen

lights up random heaps
of cold basaltic stone
waiting for their place
in the wall

last beech leaves rustle
dance loose in death

brass bell rings
across the strath
repeating
single metal notes

last remaining Christians
called to prayer

I read
Gary Snyder's *Riprap
and Cold Mountain Poems*

a pencil moves
silently
across an empty page

words
come to mind and go
together
well

the bell falls
silent

there's work to do with hands
not words

Haiku Days

Autumn wind
Leaves dancing in the sky
All day cutting wood.

Rain drilling air
Wind hammering trees
All day working words.

Blackbirds all day fighting for
Berries in the bushes
Chainsaw on the go.

Heavy clouds from the north
All day smelling the air
Snow in mind.

All day stacking logs
Rows on rows in the shed
Thinking ahead.

Aidan's Haiku

(written by my son, Aidan, aged 11)

Glowing leaves falling
Leaves glittering on the ground
A heavenly time

A Flock of Rooks

*And the old rooks that waited other springs
Have fled to stranger scenes on startled wings.*
                (John Clare, 'Round Oak and Eastwell')

A flock of rooks looking
For their rooky wood
Surveying with eye and wing
Once familiar terrain
Scoring the sky
In widening circles of
Astonishment
Arcing
Croaking
Suddenly afraid of death and bane.

The forest has fled
The trees felled
Stripped sliced and diced
And carted off to the mill
By magnified might of men
In marauding machines
Tearing out stumps and rocks
Gouging craters and bridging creeks
With mangled logs for caterpillar tracks
To trash the face of the earth,
Pumping scent of pine and pining
Into vacant air which forest filled
Just yesterday, made flying
Fun on wind-full wings
In wing-full winds
On paths of patterned light
Through trees.

Fifty years from now thousands
Of sapling oaks will form a forest
Better than ever, fit for fun and flying,
Food for fledgelings, but only if
The hungry generations in between
Make wing to find another rooky wood
To see them through.

The Fire that Never Goes Out

It's Friday night and I've got my pay
On the tramp on the moor for a weekend away,
There's rain from the west at the end of the day
But a welcome fire along the way,
On the banks of Craigallian Loch.

A tram from Glasgow, miles on foot,
And on to the fells, the loch, and the muir,
Soon we'll be wrapped in the circle of fire
And tomorrow it's on to the hills in the north,
On big tacky boots thirty miles in a day.

The night has landed and we're sitting now,
Firelight flickering on fired-up faces,
The moonlight skims on the skin of the loch
And a fresh wind blows through the ring of trees,
And man! can you smell that pure night air!

The comfort of strangers and friends for the night,
The water of life in my flask from the burn
And tea drummed up on the open fire
Take off the taste and the tang of the town,
The reek and grime of the work on the Clyde.

There's the burn for a brew, and the loch for a fish,
Take a dip in the dixie, there's stew for us all,
Tatties and turnips from fields hereabouts,
With rabbit and hare snatched with a snare,
Or venison poached from who knows where.

A magnet for meandering men like me
And women who wander away from the way,
Fugitives gathered in a circle of dreams –
Equality, fraternity,
The right to roam and freedom for all.

Drum up more tea, gather more wood,
Let's hear old timers tell of old times,
Of Craig Dhu climbers' first ascents,
Drinking, poaching, trespassing,
And fighting fascists in the mountains of Spain.

The glow of the fire holds us all in its spell
Then the stories die down and the men wrap up well
In blankets and bracken and the arms of their girls,
And suddenly all is right with the world,
For there's love on the road and life on the hills.

As the walkers and talkers settle down for the night,
There's one keeps the fire and himself to himself
He's the best of the climbers but his stories are told
By the rest of his comrades who know him of old,
His life on the road and love of the hills.

Kept alight and alive for twenty odd years,
The fire died out and the sitters departed.
But you who hike the West Highland Way
Along the side of the loch, take pause
And sit around this monument,

A fire carved out of stone that's streaked
With quartz like living flames and ringed
With a circle of words that tell the tale:
Sit here and chant the old fire chant,
Feed the fire and go your way,
Treading in footsteps of history.

ON PEOPLE IN TIME

My Father's War
Private E.T. Furniss, 5891640 (Duke of Wellington's, West Riding)

My son and I chop wood
Side by side in silence
Looking forward to winter,
The sun lies low, targets
The mountain to the north,
The sound of axe on wood
Ricochets across the strath,
Glacial, u-shaped, laced
With moraine, lateral
And terminal; the skirl
Of distant pipes and drums
Marching the mile between
War memorial and kirk,
Called by kirk bell high and clear.

My father never talked about the war
And hated those old war films on TV
In black and white, where British troops
Or the Yanks killed heroically
The German enemy. I remember
Sitting by his side in silence
Each November, on the 11th,
Wondering at his tears, watching
Him growing old and weary
Year by year. A reverent voice,
Eleven Big Ben bells ringing
Out across the land, a single cannon shot,
Two minutes' endless silence shattered
By another shot, the Last Post's

Tearful bugle notes, old comrades marching
Past the Cenotaph laying wreaths.
Medals, cap badge, stripes, and photo
Of a country boy in uniform,
Young and handsome, framed
Behind glass on a wall, and photos
Of two young men in khaki shorts,
Brothers side by side on a southern beach
Smiling, tanned, muscled,
Laid in boxes in a cupboard forever
In their prime. I imagined those two boys,
Barely out of school and basic training,
Who'd never travelled much beyond
The parish bounds, or the farm they worked,
Marching side by side across the deserts
Of North Africa, fighting
On Sicilian beaches, crossing
Apennine ridges and rivers, driving
Germans northward, liberating
Rome to cheering crowds and grateful
Girls, getting medals as they went,
A Boy's Own lark. But those annual tears,
Were shed for those who fell by the way,
Wounding him forever, his vital life
All done before I was born, leaving
The shell of a shell-shocked man.
The war was never won for him:
He fought it every day for life
Inside his head, with his wife and kids,
At war with himself and at war with us.

My son and I chop wood in silence,
Side by side.

Like Father, Like Son

For heavenly sake you say
Ignoring my correction
In moments of exasperation
Or sometimes just in play

Remember, Remember

Forty years ago today,
The day the music died,
Death of the century Havel said,
We cried for you and our lost selves.

I'm sitting down to listen once again
To your first LP record after the split,
You two lovers on the sleeve
Backs against an English oak,
Watching the English sky in pastel.

Remember, you sing –
Here and now in this room
Your voice survived the gun –
When we were young,
People seemed so tall
Made us feel small,
Crippled inside.

Like mine, your ma and pa,
Dreamt and dressed like movie stars,
One way out of working-class lives
Before rock-and-roll.

My mummy's dead
You sing at the end,
But mine was still alive
When first I heard the funeral bell
That begins your first song.

I first held this 12-inch vinyl disk
In 1970, Christmas morning,
A gift from mother still in bed,
Slipped it from the sleeve,
With its blown-up photo of a little boy
Who'd one day change the whole wide world
Emerging from the grey and grain of another time,
Listened all the way from 'Mother' to
'My Mummy's Dead' and then,
With barely a thought for my own mother, left
Our house and walked through snowy lanes
To spend a thoughtless Christmas day
With my latest, brand-new girlfriend,
The only trace of whom today
Is where she added 'fucking'
To the lyrics on the inner sleeve
Censored by the gods of E.M.I.

When I hold this relic now,
Held and wrapped by mother's hands
Fifty years ago,
And when I listen to that last bleak lovely elegiac track,
All the losses of our yesterdays
Turn, return, revolve,
Round and round again
In the dead wax run-out groove.

Lookalikes

Feeling mournful on the ninth,
December 2020,
Recalling lovers and friends
Dead and living, I read and sort
Old letters into files.

A girl called Jane I tried to bed
In my first year in hall, 1978,
Long blonde hair and eyes of blue,
Porcelain albino skin,
Sent me a Christmas greeting
Days after that terrible day:
'I've seen a picture on one of his books
Which looks very much like you.
I've not seen you since his death
And so begin to ask myself perhaps
You really are John Lennon
Leading a second quieter life
In England.' I read it
As a kind of compliment
But never replied.
I was too deep in mourning
And needed someone in my bed.

On April fifteenth, 1995,
The first day of my forty-second year,
I gave a talk on metaphor
At Rutgers University.
A bright young woman
Tall and beautiful

Said I looked like Milton with long hair.
I took it as a compliment,
But went to bed with someone else.

One of my students gave me once
A postcard of Serge Gainsbourg,
And writing on the back she said
I looked like him or he like me.
Jane Birkin thought him ugly but
She loved and lived with him, so I
Took it as a two-edged compliment
Though never went to bed with her
But fed instead my fantasies of Jane.

I look into the mirror now
And though I see vague traces of
Those three dead poets in my face
As they might have looked in age,
I'm really looking at or for
The undiscovered self I found
Or made
Through music love and poetry.

For Jason: My Close Reader

Striding down the Avenue
Dividing Southampton's woods in two
Late in the night under city lights
Elated with ourselves and wine
And being dined by first year girls
We wished to be acquainted with
The world turned beneath our feet
Now more than forty years in the past
We took the time to talk in turns
You spoke at last of Robert Frost
I listened silent as the stars
That travelled lonely tracks in the sky
And came to where two roads converge
And though we went divergent ways
That frost-filled night the days and years
And ages since revealed that we
Were treading on the self-same path
At first pursuing self-same girls
At first withholding of ourselves
But that night found profound shared love
Of poetry and friendship based
On reading closely critically
Each other's essays journals books
Heaping praise where praise is due
Unspoken promises to keep
True to the truth the ear hears
Honesty without offence
And that made all the difference.

A Season's Greetings Card from Jason and Waltraud, Christmas 2019

The equinoctial sun is an orange
Hovering low at the end of time
In this picture-postcard winter scene
That brings your season's greetings;
A shepherd wears a floppy shepherd's hat,
Crook in hand, dog at heel,
All in silhouette as winter's light
Glances off the snow into
My eyes, looking transfixed
At this levitating fruit that is the sun,
Two wind-bent leafless trees recoil
From that too-near citrus star, loom
Over the snow-roofed house whose door
Is open and whose upstairs windows
Are lit by inner light or by the muted sun
And seem to promise rest in peace
When day is done, but no smoke rises
From the chimney stack; some of the sheep
Look lost, looking askance,
Waiting for their shepherd and dog
To break their trance, some are melting
In the winter light as fields dissolve
Into the sky, four in the foreground
Stare me in the eye, soliciting
Some response, an angry ram thrusts
His curly-horned head-butting head
Into the painting, bottom left,
Demanding to be painted, about
To take charge or turn on me.

I'd never heard of Mary Fedden,
A well-loved British artist of her time,
According to the card, or seen
Her 'Winter 1995' –
On the face of it a clichéd scene
For Christmas cards but one which turns
Those clichés inside out and haunts
Me every time I look. You two live
And move and have your being
At the core of London's cultural life
And the card you chose to send to us
At the northern edges of the known world,
Like a postcard from Mars,
'Published under licence from
The Royal Academy of Arts',
Is a fitting response to the card
We sent to you, made by our son
In primary three. Yours in turn
Demanded my response, ekphrastic lines
I send to you in turn.

First Love, 1970

That sweltering summer's day at the end of school
There was one empty seat at the back of the bus,
A lower form girl I didn't know
Sitting alone. She stowed her leather satchel
And smiled. Did I ask or just sit down?
Her grey school skirt was hiked up high
On brown bare thighs, her white unbuttoned shirt
Tied in a bow to bare her waist. That old school bus
Was hot that day and she was throwing off
Constraints of school. Long waves
Of centre-parted jet-black hair
Breaking on her shoulders, dark eyes
Back lit with inner mystery, radiant
Sun-lit face, sweet sweat on brow.
Just fourteen, though I never asked.
At seventeen and never kissed,
The only way I talked to girls back then
Was to help with homework.
But she untied my tongue and so
We fell in love – first love for me – before
She left the bus in Litchborough,
A lovely village fifteen minutes from school,
And now much lovelier. That antiquated
Dusty smelly bus, the one the company
Thought fit to carry kids to school and back,
Crawled its roundabout way to
Pattishall, three miles further on,
The less-than lovely village where I lived
In my parents' rented council house.
I changed my clothes and had my tea

And then walked back on country lanes
Where sky and trees and birds on high
Were lit with loveliness and song
And met her at our rendezvous
Quite transformed. In flared jeans,
White plimsolls, soft checked shirt,
My schoolgirl was a hippy child,
Eager for love and all of life before her.
We hardly touched those first few times,
I was hesitant and shy, in awe of her,
And completely inexperienced
Save in romance of novels and words
Of Beatles' songs. When we first kissed
And first held hands, the universe
Turned for me, and the sun shone
On us alone. She took me to her secret places,
Magnetic fields where hand attracted hand,
Electric currents jumped back and forth
Between two charged electric poles,
Innocent tumescence guiltily concealed,
Impossible to imagine her desire, uncertain
How to go from there. She walked
Me part of the way back home, passing
Bluebell woods and fishing ponds; we climbed
A five-barred gate and kissed
Behind a hedge of briars entwined with wild dog-rose,
And then I would have walked her back again,
And so we would have gone on thus
For ever hand in hand. I can't remember
How we came to part, how bright
Green summer faded into autumn
And falling leaves left the season
Bereft. When I started my first job

I saw her sometimes waiting for that old school bus,
With a secret, stirring smile for me
As I glanced from the bus that took me to work,
Plying the self-same route.
But two short months had passed, it seems
In retrospect, I heard she was with child
And marrying an old schoolmate of mine
Who worked on a local farm, she
Much too young and all her golden promise
Cast away in moments of desire.
I saw her only once more after that, careworn
With a pram at a bus stop in the town.
I gave her a lift, she was going my way,
The baby quiet in the back of the car.
I left her at the gate of a terraced house
And drove away to a life that was far from there.
Did we talk of our summer of love?
Did she watch me go with a flicker of regret?
Did she think about what might have been
If I had been, at seventeen,
More versed in ways of love?

Burning Memories

Mother in a hospice bed, waning.
Not raging against the dying of the fire
But fading ever so gently,
Imperceptibly,
Into everlasting night
And permanent obscurity.
The fire burned out
That once burned bright, consumed
By that which fed it once,
A deathbed that it made itself.
Tobacco smoke burnt out her bronchioles,
Stole breath and years and hard-earned cash
For ash. In the local village church,
After the crematorium,
A small wooden box of ashes waiting
To be buried under a granite stone engraved
In consecrated earth, I raged,
In eulogy,
Against a global industry
Making a killing day by day
For decades now, smokers
In their millions, cutting
Third-world trees to burn
In drying lethal leaves.

To STC Again

We languish, you and I, in life-long loves,
Our fates almost the same,
Their first names almost perfect rhymes,
Hopeless as searching for our better selves.

Raving winds at war with trees that bend
And bow, refuse to lose their grip on earth,
The only constant in a life of change
When war in distant lands comes all too close,

Inhuman all too human, all at strife
With our best selves, the natural man,
Our shaping spirit against the worst
That our worst selves invent to break

Our spirit of resistance to invasions
Into consciousness that well up from
The depths of brains both too evolved
And hardly yet evolved enough,

That never rest in peace but undermine
Foundations of the fragile self, knowing too much
And not enough, that death will come to all
Our being and our body, but doubting whether

Being could survive the end of being,
The body's joys and jolts. We both
Have loved and lost and watched the love we loved
Live out her life alongside other love,

Haunted life-long by shapes of longing
Which nightly visit dreams forever young.
An image with a glory round her head,
Recalls that first of times her long thick blonding hair

Tangled from a day on the fells fell loose,
Unfettered and free, and eyes like pools
That held the blue of all the summer skies
We two have known invited me to drown.

Two Chained Sonnets

You were right to leave me long ago,
You found a better man, you left me free,
I've found it hard to be with me so know
There must be better ways of being me;
If I can't love this self then who would try
To hold the wind or walk upon the waves;
Light years of space expand beyond the sky
And in the I that lies inside cold caves;
But still I write this sonnet, form my verse,
To give my grief some metre, make it rhyme,
Forestall the tendency to nurse my curse –
Only thinking of you keeps me in time.
So long as I remember you as light,
I keep one step ahead of blackest night.

I keep one step ahead of blackest night
By circumnavigating east to west,
Chasing setting suns, the last of light,
Afraid of facing nights of restless rest.
And if I rested on some barren shore
And turned my back on rolling surf to stay
The night I might be overwhelmed, the roar
Might never stop. I'd have to face the day
And seek for friends and lovers without you.
The last red light is giving up the ghost.
The night you said you'd leave me then I knew
That my frail bark was given up for lost.
The polar star exploded supernova
Excess of light revealed that it was over.

Wish You Were Here

I wish I could see you,
see you today
wish I could hear you
say that you'd stay

that night you told me
you'd something to say
you said it so kindly
you were going away

as if you could fold me
and put me away
and now you inform me
you loved me that day

what are you trying
to do to me now?
I don't think you're lying
but I don't see how

to recover the years
we've wasted apart
to put away tears
re-awaken my heart

but I wish you were here
with me in my bed
I've thought of the words
I ought to have said

I wish you were here
right here by my side
nothing so near
nothing to hide

I wish you were here
we're both older now
nothing to fear
nothing to vow

I wish you were here
where you belong
or that I was there
I'd sing you this song

I wish you were here
that you'd wish it too
or I'd go anywhere
to be there with you

Rebuilding a Dry-stone Wall
(for Andy Edwards)

The dry-stone wall between my woodland
And the lower slopes of the Campsie Fells
Had not been loved for all too long. Gappings
Had been broken through along its length
By fallen trees and roots, leaping deer,
And frozen groundswells in the
Countless winters since it was built
By men who never left a name,
And here and there not one stone lay
Upon another stone.

Two years ago, or more, you offered
To help rebuild, restore that dry-stane dyke –
Just one of many crafts and skills that you
Can turn your hand to, passed on to me
By precept and example as we worked
From the ground up, stone by stone,
Hands on experience developed over time,
And what we gleaned from books, tried
And tested at the wall.

Before and between our Friday workdays
I prepared the site, chainsawing
Fallen trees straddling sections
Of wall they'd ruined. Extracting
Stumps and roots of trees that snaked
Themselves into the wall to bring about
A fall. Harvesting stones of every size
And shape with pick and bar, spade

And fork from deep leafmould soil
Built up by centuries of fallen leaves.
Gathering coping stones and heartings
From scree slopes on the hill.
Dismantling sections of the old wall
Stone by stone, with trowel and brush,
An archaeologist uncovering
Treasures from the debris of unmeasured
Time. Sorting stones by size and shape
According to their different functions
In the wall to come.

In two long lockdown years of sun and rain,
Wind and snow, and all four seasons
Sometimes in one day, we bridged
Wide gappings in three hundred yards of wall
Running west to east. Uncounted thousands
Of basalt stones forged in lava flows
That built the Fells to the north
Three hundred million years ago
We laid with care and skill, precision
And grace, into their destined place
In level courses angled to the template
Of a hand-made A-shaped batter frame
And kept in line with guidelines run
Across gappings, built upon
Foundation stones hauled
Into place with block and tackle.
Two walls of facing stones leaning
Towards each other, held apart
By in-fill heartings, held together
By friction, weight, and gravity,
Each stone bridging two below, locked

In place by two above, stabilized
With pinnings, bonded here and there
By throughstones and then crowned
With weighty coping stones lifted
With strength of sinew, ramps, and ropes.

Skills of hand and eye, body and brain,
Rhythm and flow, and thus akin
To finding fitting words for places
In a poem's line whose sound and sense
Interlocks with every other word,
Building form, structure and meaning
Greater than the sum of parts.

Working side by side or face to face
Across a wall that never came between,
Passing stones, techniques, and tools
Back and forth over its growing form,
We sometimes laboured on in quiet
Companionship, a silence broken only
By the ring of steel on stone, a hammer
Used with growing skill, or exclamations
When a long-sought stone finally fitted
An awkward place. But oftentimes the work
Was eased with talk about the work,
And talk of hills and literature,
Teaching, science, philosophy,
Memories, ideas, experience,
Children's reading, music, maths …
Building friendship on foundations that
Will last the test of time.

There's a mysterious something that I love
About our wall – I walk beside it every morning
With my dog, beating the bounds,
Admiring beauty and enduring form,
The way the countless stones of every size
And shape compose themselves into
A greater whole, a monument and legacy
Of work done for its own sake, of shared days,
And proof that building walls does not divide
Neighbour from neighbour. But best of all,
For me, the stile we built with massive
Foothold stones is often climbed by village kids
Escaping into freedom of the hills.

In Memoriam: Kenneth McNeil (20 March 1925 - 16 February 2021)

> *I climb the hill: from end to end*
> *Of all the landscape underneath,*
> *I find no place that does not breathe*
> *Some gracious memory of my friend*
> (Tennyson, *In Memoriam*)

I cannot imagine Scotland
Without your craggy face
And the mountain wind
Carrying your quiet voice across the glens
Imbuing nooks and crannies of the land
With histories that you were part of and
Were part of you.

Hiking in the Highlands with you
In gear pulled out of the cluttered museum
Of the back rooms of your house
Would, if I were lucky, draw out stories
From back pages of your life
Like glimpses of granite peaks
In the shifting canyons of cloud
Revealing threads of you within
So many strands of Scotland's woven histories.

Collective memories of working men
And Marxists on the dole,
Red Clyde-side welders, Creagh Dhu climbers,
Men and women from the Carbeth huts,
Sitting around Craigallian's never-dying fire
Listening to each other's fire-lit tales
Of first ascents and visions
Of a better future than the one we have.

Long before funicular and lifts
Made Cairngorm's northern slopes
Accessible to weekend skiers,
Along with other off-piste pioneers,
Few and far between,
You strapped mohair skins to wooden skis
And skis to hobnail leather boots, hiked
To the Ptarmigan Bowl, removed
The skins, threw caution to the howling wind,
Launched yourself into pristine wilderness,
And carved criss-crossing curves,
Sinuous sinewaves in snow,
All the way to Morlich's shore,
Then did it all again.

Not many modern skiers ski
Cross country into hidden glens for miles
Or even know about the Shelter Stone
Where long ago you skied along
Loch Avon's ice-bound length
To spend with a special woman friend.
One long-remembered New Year's Eve.

I'm almost sure you told me once
You learnt to ski cross-country
On wild slopes and trails of Telemark
In the depths of Norway's winter,
And there's no-one now to doubt the tale.

To roam with you along Glasgow's streets
Led to meetings with remarkable men
And women too – artists, teachers,
Radicals and writers from Scotland's

Eccentric, overlapping counter-cultural circles
That seemed to centre on you,
Their living link, or secret intersection
(To use the kind of language that you used).

Visits to the hubs of Glasgow's vital life
(Theatres, museums, concert halls,
Bookshops, libraries, galleries) always
Ended and began, somehow,
In those cafes, pubs, and restaurants
Where you were known by name and taste.
Vegetarian, teetotal, ascetic, of course,
You loved the true, the honest, the just,
Lovely things and things of good report,
And good food too.

You only gave out snippets
Of your quiet heroic life before we met:
Six months a prisoner of conscience
For refusing call up after the war;
A night in prison in your eighties
For 'breaching the peace' at Faslane Naval Base,
Dangerous man of peace that you were!

Years of teaching Maths in Glasgow schools
Did not deter the teacher in you:
I watched you coach and tutor everyone
Who came your way and needed help
With primary maths or PhDs
In any subject that intrigued your polymathic mind,
Quietly transforming lives.

As Wordsworth might have said of you:
The best portion of a good man's life
Is made of little, nameless,
Unremembered acts of kindness
And of love. Yet many of your kindly acts
Will be remembered by those of us
Whose lives you helped transform.

One day I found a sketch of you,
By Alasdair Gray, unsigned,
Hidden behind a wardrobe, gathering dust,
Face to the wall, hale and handsome,
Long blond flowing locks of youth.
You didn't want it signed or framed
Or hung upon a wall, saying everything
You never said about yourself.

John

Thirteen months
Was all I had at mother's breast
Before you came along
Out of nowhere
To take my place,
Push me out in the cold
On my father's bony knee.
Thirteen months
Ahead of you
In walking and talking,
Precociously of course,
To demonstrate
That I'd always be ahead.
All of this remained unsaid
Unthought
To the end,
Yet somehow we became
After you were weaned
Playmates
As well as brothers.
We shared
A second-hand old double bed
Sunday night baths
And that wild triangle
Of grass and weeds outside
The kitchen door
For making up games,
And ventured forth
In fields and woods
And farmers' barns

Beyond the garden fence,
Helped with baling
And silage making,
Rode out on bikes
That shook our bones,
Made sledges in the winter
Of 1963,
Played hide and seek
Among the graves across the road,
Climbed trees, built dens
Damned streams and fished
In ponds and gathered leaves
To flesh out Guy Fawkes
Every year to burn
In our garden,
Played with bat and ball
In hallway, field, and once
One glorious summer eve
Out on the road
When all the parents in the village
It seemed
Joined us in an endless game,
Stumps chalked on the vicarage wall.
Only the occasional car and fallen night
Stopped play that day.
I never knew you treasured that game,
As I did,
For sixty years,
Until we finally talked
Days before you died,
About the life we shared
In that rural council house
Your first ten years before

We were wrenched away
(It seemed to us)
To an alien house in a foreign land
(One mile down the road
Across Watling Street),
The house where you would live
(But never love, you told us
At the end)
For all the years that you had left to live,
Where we had single beds in separate rooms
And different schools
And different friends
And set out on our different ways
Until we only met as strangers
Under that roof
Or out on the tiles.
And when your brothers flew
That troubled nest, you remained,
Nursed mother in her final months,
Coexisted with 'the old man'
You hated from a child
(You told us why, or some of it,
On that last day)
Until he died in a home from home
And the house was yours.
Thereafter there was never a word
From you, one year to the next
And only gruff rebuffs –
'What the bloody hell are you doing here?'
Whenever I came to knock on your door.
And so it was until I found out
You were dying in the hospice
Where mother died of the same disease

From the same cause;
And so we met for the final time
Both nervously
On a warm spring day in May
On the terraced roof where the nurses let you smoke
(Against the rules – but no point giving up
When the body's given up on you)
In a wheelchair face to face,
Eye to eye,
Your body, once so strong,
Ever ready for a fight,
Hard-worked over years,
Giving way, but not your mind,
Not your humour, unique
And wholly you,
And so we laughed a lot
And cried;
You'd had a good life you said
(Too short I thought),
Were not afraid of death,
And your humanity
Hidden all those years behind facades
Of tough-guy masculinity
Broke out as tears when I produced
A long-lost photograph,
Saved when mother's things were cleared,
Your only daughter's only son
Who died an infant in his cot
Many years ago,
Unashamed to show, at last,
Capacity to love and grieve.
I found my long-lost brother at the last
A few short hours almost wiped away

Those lost decades.
I never saw you more, that was that,
Except I saw still more of you
In the host of friends who came
To see you off, a village
Toasting you with beer and wine
At your expense,
The biggest round you ever bought,
In the last remaining village pub
Of the many where you drank
Your fill of life.

LOCKDOWN TIME

April Moon, 2020

Invisible worms hollow the night
Blight the sight of bright moonlight
Dark secret bane on human breath
Radiates our breathless death
Sleepless now self-isolating
Fearing what the day will bring.

Biggest brightest moon of the year
A microscope examining our fear
Daylight at the heart of night
Illuminates those heartless heights
That loom above our glacial glen
And lure us from the world of men,
Mountains move, the old world rolls
From west to east the star screen scrolls
Majestic midnight cloudless eye
Silences owls and empties the sky
Of bats and all but the brightest stars
And the unblinking stare of marauding Mars.

Never the mother of pathos and pity,
Laughable credulity,
We know you're dead and made of dust
Your rocks are just the same as us
Without a molten heart to move
Your surface calm and therefore prove
That you can feel what poets claim
For life on earth, this goodly frame,
Our sole companion as we race
In endless circuits of empty space

Tied with bonds we can never sever
Dancing forever in circles together
Month by month and year by year
You only appear to disappear,
Wax and wane and tug our tides
Hide in shame your nether side,
Two hundred thousand miles away
Not thirty earths between us today
This is the closest I'll ever come
To writing your encomium.

But why would I apostrophise
A barren rock in cavernous skies
In this our hour of greatest need
Why revert to an outworn creed?
Why do you lurk in the heartless night
Why so cold and eye so bright
Spying on our mirthless mirth
On the dark side of the earth
Waiting out the silent night
To give to spring its ancient rite?

My son is sleeping by my side
Untroubled by the swelling tide
Let him wander like the breeze
That rattles our budding woodland trees
Let him and schoolfriends come through this
Experience later love's first bliss
Out in the hills and under the moon
Let us out of lockdown soon.

Glen Lyon, October 2020

Our ten-year old VW estate
Carries us and our bikes with ease
Into the depths of this Highland glen,
Long, lonely, lovely,
First surveyed and mapped by Pont
Four hundred years ago.
We spare no thought for the cost
Of the last hundred years or more
Of making cars or maybe millions
Of trees that made the wheels
That rolled the world before,
Or rainforests cleared to make
These high-tech tyres that run so smooth
On a road first driven into this glen
By military might to map
And master mountains and men
And clear the clans that made last stands
Against modernity,
Campbells and MacGregors.

Ordnance Survey maps and apps
From outer space now open up
This land, surveying every untamed inch,
Making sure that no one goes
Astray or loses themselves
In wilderness. Two centuries
Of bicycle technology
Went into the making
Of these high-tech mountain bikes
We ride along an off-road track,

Revealed on a tattered OS map
Landranger 51,
A quarter of an inch to every mile,
That runs from Invervar
To Bridge of Balgie
Along the south bank of the Lyon
Linking farms to farms and gated
Every now and then and fenced
To keep the deer on the hills
And out of valley fields
Made by glaciers and men
Who hauled out stones to wall
The land by laying craftfully
Stones on stones, and bridged
Burns tumbling from the crags.
Such engineering skill and history
And all the human labour
That reshaped these hills made possible
At the end of lockdown summer
Our release into this broad glen,
Farmed and forested for centuries,
Captured instantly now
By camera apps on mobile phones,
Yet still with traces of old
Wilderness: ancient Caledonian
Forest remnants cling to flanks
Of mountains looming in sun-lit mist.
Red deer stags rut and roar.
Land Drover driving keepers pass
In masks, dead stags in the back,
Culled from the hills. A woman
Keeps her baby close to her chest,
Walks between farms. Sheepdogs bark.

We hardly knew we were biking
One of Scotland's ancient, storied glens,
Peopled in prehistory, a place
Of wood and stone, bronze and iron;
We missed the cairns, stone circles,
Standing stones, the shrine
To Cailleach, creator goddess of the Celts,
Saw no sign that Adomnán
Abbot of Iona often came this way,
Fourteen hundred years ago,
Heading towards the pagan north,
Saving local pagans as he went
With miracles that banished the plague.

The Gift of Poetry

Everything comes to those who wait
for the end
no more getting and spending
but click and collect,
click and deliver,
a ring of the bell
parcels at the door.
Zoom and WhatsApp link
isolating selves in webs
of social distance,
locked down in the internet.
Even poems are sometimes delivered
gratis, unordered, gifted
from an unknown source:
at the typeface early today
straight to screen
before I entered the password
one of those stunning scenes
I barely glance at when I feel
a poem is on its way
but there it was
a morning desktop background
I hadn't seen before
a place I've never been
except on screen
in Kassel Germany
domed white classical temple
fake of course
on margins of a lake
trees artfully arranged

with poetic words as well:
*a channel of water here cascades
through falls and rapids to a lake
where it erupts in a geyser after
moments of reflection at
the water's edge near Apollo's Temple.*
These words and image came
more easily than leaves to a tree: but whence
and why to me remains a mystery.
Eruptions of a geyser used to be
an image for how poetry seems to come
unbidden from some inner depth,
and moments of reflection
(I like the double meaning) was one too.
That's not really Apollo's temple, of course,
the god of poetry resides in ancient Greece.
I suppose this morning's desktop image
came from Microsoft or Dell
selected by A.I. at random from
a memory bank in the cloud. I took it
as a gift of poetry.

Spring 2021
(After Tu Fu)

In this land, only the land itself
Seems firm, though even the soil
Is made from mountains weathering
And mountains are continually made
By movements underground.

It is springtime in the city
And no one tends the parks and gardens anymore,
But your weeds are my wildflowers
Watered by April rains and all the trees
Are free at last to reach for the sky
And shelter singing birds.

Beacon fires no longer burn on mountain peaks
These days, signalling emergencies,
And no one waits for letters anymore;
Words and images are whirled around the world,
From satellite to satellite,
Faster than the speed of thought,
Linking all the people in a web of lies
And viral stories of the plague infect our minds
And nothing that we read is worthy of our trust,
For no one now has time for poetry
Such as yours.

We too have wars, of course,
That rage and range across the world,
But though our weapons would blanch your old white hair
We are now at war with living forms too small to see,

That you, great poet though you were,
Never imagined, that may kill more perhaps
Than all our wars combined.

But it's spring at last and in this land
The plague that flies on the wind from breath to breath,
That killed two hundred thousand of our citizens
In eighteen months, is dying back.
In other lands the war goes on and bodies burn.

Ash to Ash

Fraxinus in silvis pulcherrima (Virgil, *Eclogues*, VII, 65)

Yes, the ash was once in Virgil's time,
And in our own, the fairest tree
In the woodlands of our land.
Hopkins' ash boughs were the best
Milk to the mind. If half of Thomas's
Grove stood dead, those that lived
Recalled a song soft as love
Uncrossed. But more than half of all
Our groves are dead or dying now,
Though not yet massacred to the last ash.

No longer hemmed and starved of light
And nutriment by densely planted
Spruce and larch that seven years
Ago were felled and lie in stacks
Of logs and wait for saw and axe
To cut and split and heat the house
For winters to come, the ash trees on
Our land are free to reach for the sky
And spread themselves. And yet, bereft,
Exposed, and branchless almost to
The crown and almost leafless late
In May, except for scattered shoots
Springing here and there from trunk
And branches, dropping firewood for
Pit and stove, they're looking less
And less like themselves, less and less
Like those by Constable.

Ash are often late, even behind
The oak this year; old country-folk
Would see a long dry summer coming:
Oak before ash, only a splash
Ash before oak, surely a soak.
But I am looking for other signs
Unknown to woodland lore – dieback
Of the crown, necrotic xylem
Lesions, diamond wounds where branch
Meets trunk and branches turning purple,
And darkling blotches on early leaves,
Epicormic growth from dormant
Buds along the trunk, symptoms
Of dieback ash disease,
Hymenoscyphus fraxineus,
Invasive fungoid pathogens
That stowed away on Asian saplings
Imported who knows why,
Unlikely ever to leave or die,
Killing old and vulnerable trees.

Our native ash were said to cure
Diseases, ward off evil spirits,
Absorb shocks that would splinter
Other woods, but can't defend
Themselves against exploding fungus
Spores that spread on summer winds,
Tracked and traced by the Woodland Trust.

The old rhyme truly says that ash
Is best for burning even green.
In our rusted firepit bowl,
Tripodal, circular, branches

That fell before their time, cut
Into logs or cut to stem disease,
Burn ever brighter in summer gloaming,
Fanned by intermittent breeze
Through narrow elliptic pinnate leaves
Of trees that now will never reach
A grand old age, slowly dying
On their feet, hollowed out hearts
Sapping the will to live. Sudden
Changes of wind blow smoke in eyes
That watch embers ashen and glow,
Reigniting memories
Of self-consuming fire dying
Like a dying star.

There is no cure for infected trees.
Spores pass from tree to tree
With high infection rates, changing
Forests, hedgerows, skies forever,
Making the past a place we'll never
Forget or find again, leaving
Skeletons of once great trees
As monuments. In future children
Might never see an ash in leaf,
Their unkempt crowns ruffled in wind,
Or fronds of pointed oval leaves
Laced upon the sky, seeking
After the sun like Blake's sunflower,
Reaching for heaven, or see their seeds
Enclosed in winged keys, spiralling
In autumn winds, or hear again
The clash of the ash.

We could not well have a wagon,
A cart, a coach or wheelbarrow,
A plough, a harrow, a spade, an axe
Or hammer if we had no ash.

William Cobbett was right in his day
And partly so in ours. It's still
The wood of choice for handles of
Hammers, axes, spades, and forks,
For harrows, hop-poles, hurdles, hoops,
Wheelbarrows, ladders, and other kinds
Of agricultural plenishings.
It's best for oars and hockey sticks,
Catapults, bows, and arrow shafts.
And charcoal made from slowly burning
Ash in earth-covered clamps is best
For sketching trees and human faces.

Perhaps the ash will only survive
In poetry and myth, the space
Where medicine and magic meet,
Burned to ward off evil spirits,
Of great virtue against warts and bite
Of serpents, once the wood of choice
For druids' wands and spear of Odin,
Tree of life and core of the world
And universe, reaching for heaven
And rooted deep in the underworld,
Like us. When the ash dies all life
Will die – so says the myth.

The embers in the firepit have
Died down. The ash of all that ash
Barely fills the bowl and blows
On the wind that carries spoors
And viruses that seek the weak
Points in our trees' immunity
And our humanity.

And yet there's hope the ash will rise,
Phoenix-like, to brighten the lives
Of children of our children. Some
Appear immune, the fittest survive,
Like 'Betty' in a Norfolk wood,
Pass on their DNA in scattered seeds
And seedlings nursed by front-line staff
Of the Woodland Trust.

Mycorrhizal Fungi

If I should fall in this war of the world
Against this virus that has felled so many,
Ruining the landscapes of the present
And the past, as ash are dying
From a disease already wrecking
The woodlands of our lives,
Remember this of me – my love
Has only grown over the years,
Adding extra layers ring by ring,
Season by season. Trees, I've read,
Have secret lives, live better side by side
Than those who stand alone
And only have fresh air, good soil,
All the rain and shine they need,
And cattle making manure under their shade.
Companion trees grow closer
Over centuries, silently commune,
Exchange subtle messages through
Entangled roots or through the air
They share, mutually beneficial
Symbiosis between fine fibres
Of roots and mycorrhizal fungi –
Ancient arboreal internet and web.

After forty silent years, which is
Nothing to a tree, I.T. makes possible
New kinds of intimate exchange
Through fibre networks underground,
Electromagnetic waves in the air,
And new attachments (poems

And photographs of our shared past),
Stirring old roots, feeding
Fresh shoots, reviving dormant
Connections, unearthing deep
Entanglements that formed themselves
Beyond our ken, unconscious
Pheromonal interchange, apocrine
Secretions, fluid communications
Subtler than words, even in poems,
Could convey.

MOMENTS OF BEING

On An Ordinary August Day

In the kitchen, door open wide
To trees, sweet air, summer sun,
My son and I calm at culinary tasks,
When out of the blue a dark
Cloaked alien being burst
The invisible barrier between
Out and in, wild and tame,
Raw and cooked, a whirling blur
Crashing crazed wings against
Dishwasher, fridge, cupboards,
Oven, worktop, walls, doors,
Battering frantically
At windows over the sink,
Freedom of woods and air and sun
Just beyond transparency bafflingly solid,
Glass not glazed into instinct
By millions of years of flight
In open air. Finally netting
All that explosive energy
Trembling in my hands, balsa light,
Suddenly calm, I carried it out
The way it came and flung into the air
A blackbird once again. Inside,
Breast feathers litter the floor
And my son's first telling of the story,
Of the wild thing and thrill
Of fear and joy that entered
An open door and electrified
Our nerves and how his father
Took it in his hands and launched it
Into the sky.

Magnetic Movements

some moments are magnetically
held in mind as more
than memories they draw
me and I draw them
more than mimetically
gigantically
like mountains of the mind
that loom more magically
than those we climbed
through heather together
and when I go there later
I find there's nothing I can find
that is more dear
closer to fate or
more near
than those places in perpetual past
that will last
while mind holds fast
to body's tether
whether or not
afterlife or nothing is our lot.

Winter

Winter trees whipped by winter wind
Whipping wintry air, silhouetted
By glimmers of winter sun, flecks
Of snow in my eyes, that smell of northern hills
And the icing of the lake's meniscus
Creeping out of the east from Russian steppes
And the crows and rooks flung about
In the buoyant air surfing simply
For the joy of it and me just walking
On and on on the moor just
For the joy of it and air in lungs.

Golden River

River runs shallow after a spell
Of dry sun-lit days in March
Luminous in morning light
Bed of golden stone more precious
Than panned metal trembling
Surface skin reflecting billions
Of photons through narrow straights
Of eyes to set me glowing.
Sunday bell appeals to me
Across the flat lit land
Summoning at speed of sound
Remembrance of time past
Just beyond the riverbend.
My dog, colour of riverbed
Flecked with fox-red sand, plunges
Through air and water and light
Driven by impulse beyond control
Ingrained in generations' genes
To retrieve thrown sticks like shot birds
Fallen from the sky, drags
The sun in her wake, tosses
A rainbow around her head
Casts with waving tail lit droplets into
Solar powered sinewaves
Blazing trails of glory.

On Listening Once Again to Beethoven's Piano Concerto No.4

A single note, long waited for
Can break your heart
Or make it whole again
Not just that note alone
But the silence between notes
What went before
And what it promises
Its leap up the scale
And half a second's delay
Catching breath,
                suspending
Melody and being
In mindless mindfulness
And longing for it to sound again
For the work it does
In the repair shop of the soul
If we can call it that
Who only know of soul
When ascending notes
Lift us soulless
Into soulfulness.

Poem Craft

Chopping wood for winter,
Stacking the woodshed.
Mending dry stone wall,
Placing stones in places
They seem destined for
Through eras and eons
Of being formed, deformed,
Reformed, displaced
By folding, fire and flood,
Each stone locking
Adjacent stones in place
And locked in place in turn
With neighbour stones,
Through-stones, copers.
Making paths through woodland,
Tilling soil for sowing seeds,
Choosing, chopping, changing,
Stacking, mending, bridging,
Placing words in place, making
Paths through word-land ways
Which travellers may tread,
And readers read.

Sonnet

Thoughts arise like passing wind-blown waves
That flit across the surface of a pond
And when they shape themselves as images
For drafts of drafts of poems, breezes die,
Meniscus once more mirrors perfectly
The high blue empty depthless sky and eye,
And when I seek profundity of depths,
The deeper the darker, or surfaces of heaven
High above, one photon in the dark,
A billion in the sunlit air, appear
Alike like inner light, but when I rise
Gasping for breath, grasping at the light,
It slips through fingers, drops into the pond,
Neither sounds the depths nor makes a sound.

Tree

From sapling to strapping giant
In just two hundred years
Running rings around yourself
Rooting deep and branching out
Aiming high and budding
Ever more profusely
Always young when getting old
Birthing and girthing yourself
Turning over new leaves
Every spring and burying them
In the fall to nurture yourself,
Weaving nets of branches
For birds to perch and nest
And offering leaves to all
The sects of insect life
To take up home and feed
The fledglings till they launch
Themselves onto the buoyant
Air to sink or swim
Swaying with the blows that come
Out of the blue and the west
Weaving underground networks
Conspiring on common grounds
With long-time neighbours round about
Of various shapes and hues
With evocative names to bind
The larger landscapes with
Your interactive beauty
Generating solar power
To split the C from CO^2

The chemical reaction
That helps you build yourself
And all the building blocks
Of life on earth, giving life
Even in death, and when you fall
Eventually a natural burial
Will enrich the soil for saplings
To root and branch and reach for the sky.

Blane Water

it's almost certain some of the molecules
of H^2O now mingling in the waters
of the Blane flowing under the bridge
at the bottom of our road once jostled in
the river outside Troy that almost drowned
Achilles; perhaps less likely that this river
which follows my daily walk is partly composed
of water from that flood which drowned the world
for the sins of men in ancient myth, and later
flowed through the river pool in which John dipped
the son of man; but some of it must have tumbled
out of the highest mountains in the world
and lost itself in the Ganges many times
to purify the bodies of the dead,
releasing souls from endless rounds of birth
and death; hydrologic cycles have gyred
the planet's water since it first appeared on earth
perhaps from outer space; here inner space
can be explored watching the river flow
where writings of the world can circulate
and it's worth knowing just downstream from here
the village sewage works distils pure water
from our excremental waste and pumps
it in the Blane; we are excreting bodies
not just souls yet poetry flows on
in a million channels endlessly recycling
images from *Iliad*, from *Gita*,
and the ancient dreams of Israel.

Climbing Trees

I climbed a tree today – I'm
only seventy after all, and
there was no one else around,
only my dog – not all the way
to the top you understand but
elevation quite enough
to see familiar land
in unfamiliar ways
to feel that climbing joy
I haven't felt since I was a boy
and instantly there and then,
another country and another time
intruded itself, into my mind,
the here and now,
the earthy smell of sycamore leaves
on the cusp of autumn,
the rhythm of hands and feet
on branches of a tree
that normally
I get my dog to climb
to reach, at the furthest limit
of a long walk, the stick
she has retrieved all the way
to here, a tree that climbs itself
of course, reaching to surrender,
expanding its girth like me until
it's time to fall, but here right now,
down there, my dog looks up
askance at me
behaving beyond

all bounds of precedence
disturbing the order of things,
whines, walks away,
and wanders in a circle round
the trunk, nose to the ground,
and looks around in puzzlement
when I call her name, ecstatic
when I've come down to earth
where I belong, where men
of seventy ought to stay
when all is right with the world,
and so we turn for home
as we always do at this tree,
our turning point,
but as we play again our game
of sticks I'm still back there
high in that tree,
still the boy somewhere
who used to sway at the tops of trees
that leant with the wind,
gazing beyond the limits of my world
reaching for the sky.

Autumn In the Garden of Delight

In the greenhouse, late cherry red tomatoes
Burst on my tongue, juice of life conjures
Ungraspable memories, smell
Of broken foliage lingers on fingers
Pinching out shoots that spurt
Between stem and branch carried on streams
Of air flowing through nasal cavities to lungs
And heart and blood pulses through veins
To limbs and all extremities and innermost
Circumnavigation makes
The turning world turn back.

On the south-facing bench by the dry-stone wall,
At the upper limit of our land, light
Of low northern sun skims the hills
At the southern rim of the strath, floods
Eyes, bones of my face, irradiates
All inner space, whole body full of light
Cast from the single eye of a star
93 million miles from where I sit,
Being here and now. Rustle of late leaves,
Flight of birds from tree to tree, sounds
Surfing wave upon wave of compressed air
That stroke taut drums of ears, making
This corporeal self an instrument of delight,
And press of skin on worked wood, touch
Of hand on rock, dispatch electric messages
Through spinal cord to brain and ground
Me in my being else I might be lost to me
And to this outer world, source of all the joy
Of being me.

JUST MY FUN

Suppose there is no secret after all,
But only just my fun.

(Christina Rossetti, 'Winter: My Secret')

Big Shots

You think you're a big shot strutting
Around my garden like you own
The place, poking your nose
Wherever it's not wanted, posing
For the camera, sunlight shimmering
In that gaudy plumage you're so proud
To wear, my blue-headed, red-eyed,
Long-tailed, weak-winged,
All-too common,
Fine-feathered friend.

Although you are undoubtedly
The finest, fairest bird in the land,
Though not the brightest, familiar
To all who love the country,
You're a foreigner, my friend, or
Come from foreign stock, despite
Your ancient lineage:
You came in with the conqueror
To occupy the land you think you own
And one day soon you'll get yours yet.

You think you're safe in the woods,
Deep in the thicket; but beaters will come
When it's open season on you
And then you'll find that you can barely fly
Above the canopy, and big shots
From near and far will fill the empty air,
Heather, trees, and bracken, full of lead,
And you'll be dead or dying in the mouths of dogs,
Beyond all care.

Three days hung by the neck till you stink
And then plucked and guts wrenched
From your belly and fed to the dogs,
Then trussed and stuffed and roasted,
According to one of many recipes
That cook only knows, and carved
With many a lame jest before those big shots
Stuff you and the lead-shot in your flesh
Into slobbering mouths still hot,
Washed down into their guts with wine
To fortify their blood-shot veins and self-belief.

For the Birds

Not exactly birds of a feather,
They never flocked in public at least
But often gathered for variegated feasts.
Tom, Jenny, Robin, and Jack
And Maggie too in her finery
Repaired to the highest vantage point
Of the upmost branch of the tallest tree
Where Jack had made a nest of sticks
Chewing over remains of the day
Wondering where the light went when
It sank in the west. But one day Robin
Turned on Tom and drove him from
The garden, Jack was seen to steal
Jenny's eggs and share them with
His in-law daws, and Maggie went
To strut her stuff, ravishing
And cruel, hopping, skipping, jumping,
On the hunt for one of her kind
And all things bright and beautiful.
And so the fellowship broke in pieces
Each one took to his own species
Some expanded, some diminished
Some have flourished, some are almost
Finished. But this is not a story
Of the birds you'll find in songs of bards.
It has its roots in common words
Inherited from country folk
Who knew the ways of birds and men.
Call it a story of natural selection
Of friendship's evolution

From a garden in common
To enmity and strife and so
A parable of human life
And in the end a play of words.

Compost

The dead poets compost down
In a delicate balance of green and brown
I turn them often in my mind
Turn their pages and I find

They add new life to rows of words
Give new voice to choirs of birds
Enrich the soil for turning worms
And the sense of worming turns

A Knight's Strange Night

(for my son aged 9)

A knight rode long and hard through the night,
Knee-deep on his horse though rivers,
He knew when the new day came at last
His fate would be decided.

When the sun rose, he fell to his knees,
Laid his head on his knapsack and napped,
Woke to the knell of a bell in the forest
And the kiss of rain on his face.

He led his horse by the reins for an hour
And came to a cottage in a dell,
He knocked with his knuckles on the wooden door
And heard strange sounds inside.

Out came an ancient knock-kneed woman
Who said he wasn't welcome there;
He said he needed to break his fast
And he could give her gold.

She stood aside, he stepped inside,
A fire burnt in the hearth,
She took a knife and cut some bread
And filled a glass with ale.

While he ate his bread and drank his fill
She sat by the fire to knit,
Then needing more bread, she kneaded some dough
And placed it by the fire to rise.

The sated knight soon fell asleep,
She bound him fast with rope,
She had a knack for secret knots
That only she could tie.

When the knight awoke, he was alone,
Cold on the cold-stone floor,
He couldn't move his hands to reach
The knife that hung from his belt.

The knocker sounded on the cottage door
He cried aloud for help,
A damsel came and loosed the knots,
That only she knew how.

Young she was and beautiful,
He thanked her with a kiss,
They stirred the embers in the grate
And burnt the cottage down.

He knelt before her on his knees,
And promised to protect her,
She took him up on her prancing horse,
And galloped far way.

That knight and lady tied the knot,
The wedding bell rang out,
A death knell echoed through the wood
But no one knows who for.

Acknowledgements

I would like to express my thanks to Ian Gouge for assisting with the publication of this collection.

www.ingramcontent.com/pod-product-compliance
Lightning Source LLC
Chambersburg PA
CBHW072212070526
44585CB00015B/1311